Upper Columbia Basin Network Stream Channel Characteristics and Riparian Condition Annual Report 2010

UPPER COLUMBIA
BASIN NETWORK

John Day Fossil Beds National Monument (JODA)

Natural Resource Data Series NPS/UCBN/NRDS—2011/181

Eric N. Starkey
Aquatic Biologist
Upper Columbia Basin Network- Inventory and Monitoring Program
105 E. 2nd St.
Suite #7
Moscow, ID 83843

August 2011

U.S. Department of the Interior
National Park Service
Natural Resource Stewardship and Science
Fort Collins, Colorado

The National Park Service, Natural Resource Stewardship and Science office in Fort Collins, Colorado publishes a range of reports that address natural resource topics of interest and applicability to a broad audience in the National Park Service and others in natural resource management, including scientists, conservation and environmental constituencies, and the public.

The Natural Resource Data Series is intended for the timely release of basic data sets and data summaries. Care has been taken to assure accuracy of raw data values, but a thorough analysis and interpretation of the data has not been completed. Consequently, the initial analyses of data in this report are provisional and subject to change.

All manuscripts in the series receive the appropriate level of peer review to ensure that the information is scientifically credible, technically accurate, appropriately written for the intended audience, and designed and published in a professional manner. Data in this report were collected and analyzed using methods based on established, peer-reviewed protocols and were analyzed and interpreted within the guidelines of the protocols.

Views, statements, findings, conclusions, recommendations, and data in this report do not necessarily reflect views and policies of the National Park Service, U.S. Department of the Interior. Mention of trade names or commercial products does not constitute endorsement or recommendation for use by the U.S. Government.

This report is also available from the Upper Columbia Basin Network (http://www.nature.nps.gov/im/units/ucbn/) and the Natural Resource Publication Management website (http://www.nature.nps.gov/publications/nrpm/) on the internet.

Please cite this publication as:

Starkey, E. N. 2011. Upper Columbia Basin Network stream channel characteristics and riparian condition annual report 2010: John Day Fossil Beds National Monument (JODA). Natural Resource Data Series NPS/UCBN/NRDS—2011/181. National Park Service, Fort Collins, Colorado.

NPS 177/109164, August 2011

Contents

Figures

Tables

Appendices

Executive Summary

The mission of the National Park Service is "to conserve unimpaired the natural and cultural resources and values of the national park system for the enjoyment of this and future generations" (NPS 1999). To uphold this goal, the Director of the NPS approved the Natural Resource Challenge to encourage national parks to focus on the preservation of the nation's natural heritage through science, natural resource inventories, and expanded resource monitoring (NPS 1999). Through the Challenge, 270 parks in the national park system were organized into 32 inventory and monitoring networks.

The Upper Columbia Basin Network (UCBN) has identified 14 priority park vital signs, indicators of ecosystem health, which represent a broad suite of ecological phenomena operating across multiple temporal and spatial scales. Our intent has been to come up with a balanced and integrated "package" of vital signs that meets the needs of current park management, but will also be able to accommodate unanticipated environmental conditions in the future. Stream channel characteristics and riparian condition are a particularly high priority vital sign for five of the nine UCBN parks. The UCBN contains more than 34 rivers, streams, ponds and reservoirs located in nine park units spread over four large western states. Unlike many National Parks that are large and often encompass entire watersheds, most UCBN parks and water bodies are small and embedded in large watersheds with diverse land use. Stream channel and riparian conditions in most UCBN streams have not been directly assessed.

Data from the 2010 field sampling effort was collected following methods detailed in the UCBN stream channel characteristics and riparian condition monitoring protocols (Starkey et al. 2011, Starkey et al. 2010) and the United States Forest Service- PACFISH/INFISH Biological Opinion (PIBO) peer reviewed protocols (Heitke et al. 2009, Leary and Ebertowski 2010). The UCBN stream channel characteristics protocol was formally peer-reviewed and approved for implementation in December 2010. This protocol can be found on the UCBN website at: http://science.nature.nps.gov/im/units/ucbn/reports/index.cfm#IWQ_Mon. The UCBN riparian condition protocol was submitted for peer review in August 2010 and is currently undergoing minor revisions.

Note that field work for this protocol is completed by PIBO through an interagency agreement with the UCBN. Benthic macroinvertebrates were also collected by PIBO according to their peer reviewed protocol (Heitke et al. 2009). Results of macroinvertebrate sampling are reported in the UCBN integrated water quality annual report 2010 for JODA (Starkey 2011).

This annual report details the status of key stream channel characteristics and riparian attributes obtained from the first season of monitoring in the John Day River within the Sheep Rock unit of John Day Fossil Beds National Monument (JODA). This report is intended as a release of basic data sets and data summaries. Care has been taken to assure accuracy of raw data values, but thorough analysis and interpretation of the data has not been completed. More extensive analysis and discussion of stream channel characteristics and riparian will occur as part of the trend analysis, which will be available after 3 years of monitoring data become available.

Acknowledgments

Funding for this project was provided through the National Park Service Natural Resource Challenge and the Servicewide Inventory and Monitoring Program. We would like to thank the PACFISH/INFISH- Biological Opinion Effectiveness Monitoring Program (PIBO-EM) for their many contributions to the UCBN stream channel characteristics and riparian condition protocols. Their willingness to collaborate with regional partners will greatly contribute to the understanding of water resources throughout the region.

Introduction and Background

In 2010, the UCBN began its first year of stream channel characteristics and riparian condition monitoring in the John Day River at John Day Fossil Beds National Monument (JODA). Stream channel characteristics and riparian condition have been identified as a high priority vital sign in the Upper Columbia Basin Network (UCBN). Stream channel and bank morphology, stability, and composition are fundamental and directly measurable attributes of lotic systems that directly affect riparian vegetation, water quality, and aquatic fauna, particularly macroinvertebrates and fish (Garrett et al. 2007). Water resources, including channels and riparian plant communities, in the semi-arid west have been strongly affected by human activity (Elmore and Kauffman 1994), streams within the UCBN are of no exception. Most UCBN streams and their aquatic resources such as migratory fish are strongly influenced by activities in the larger watersheds outside park boundaries. Understanding the current status of freshwater ecosystems will help guide management and restoration efforts, and provide insight into ecosystem change in a landscape with changing climate and dynamic human influences.

As many authors have noted, there is an intimate connection between stream channels and the surrounding landscape (Gregory et al. 1991, Elmore and Kauffman 1994, Richards et al. 1996, Rosgen 1996, Sweeney et al. 2004). Stream channels are a product of regional geomorphology, hydrology, riparian vegetation, upland vegetation, land use and water use. Within a stream, channel characteristics profoundly influence habitat for macroinvertebrates and fish. This connection between the surrounding landscape, stream channels, and aquatic habitat makes monitoring channel characteristics and riparian condition an important aspect of natural resource monitoring in the UCBN.

Well articulated desired future condition statements have not yet been developed for stream channel characteristics or riparian condition in UCBN parks. However, the mission statements for the NPS as a whole and for the individual parks clearly state the intent "to conserve unimpaired the natural and cultural resources and values of the national park system for the enjoyment of this and future generations" (NPS 1999). Stream channels and riparian areas are of particularly high importance due to their connection to both aquatic and terrestrial ecosystem health, as well as their impact on cultural resources. It is assumed that desired future conditions for all UCBN parks will include streams and rivers that support natural processes, and provide visitors with recreational and scenic experiences. By monitoring stream channel characteristics and riparian condition we will be directly measuring attributes important to park mission, visitor experience, and desired future conditions.

Objectives

The overarching programmatic goal of the UCBN Stream Channel Characteristics and Riparian Condition Monitoring Protocols is to obtain information that will aid management and restoration decisions pertaining to stream channels and riparian areas within UCBN parks. The primary objective of current stream channel and riparian management in UCBN parks is to prevent extensive changes from that of historic condition and to restore stream channels and riparian communities, if necessary, to maintain a system with biotic integrity and good hydrologic function.

Stream Channel Characteristics

Given the lack of available data on channel characteristics in UCBN parks, the following fundamental questions drive much of the UCBN's inquiry.

- Are stream channel attributes improving or degrading over time?
- Do planform and cross section measures collected within UCBN streams indicate changes in landuse or management practices?
- How do UCBN stream channel conditions compare to those in the watershed and region?
- Do cross section measures collected within UCBN streams indicate impaired habitat for macroinvertebrates or fishes?
- Are cultural resources at risk of degradation due to stream bank erosion?

In light of these questions and the broader goals outlined above, this protocol addresses the following specific measurable monitoring objectives:

- Determine the status of bank stability, percent undercut, bank angle, percent fines, and other key stream channel characteristics for selected wadeable stream reaches.
- Determine the direction and magnitude of change over time for bank stability, percent undercut, bank angle, percent fines, and other key stream channel characteristics, and establish whether those changes reflect impacts from management or land use activities.
- Determine the condition of key stream channel attributes within selected wadeable UCBN stream reaches, relative to PACFISH/INFISH Biological Opinion Effectiveness Monitoring Program (PIBO) sample reaches in the same watershed.
- Determine if changes in stream channels, specifically bank erosion, are likely to negatively impact cultural resources within the floodplain.

Riparian Condition

Given the lack of available data on riparian condition (Table 1; Figure 4) in UCBN parks, the following fundamental questions drive much of the UCBN's inquiry.

- What is the status of biotic integrity and hydrologic function of UCBN riparian zones?
- What is the direction and magnitude of change in UCBN riparian zone condition, as indicated by greenline and channel cross-section measures of vegetation cover collected along select UCBN streams?

- How do UCBN riparian conditions compare to those in the watershed and region?
- Do cover measures collected along UCBN streams indicate impaired habitat for macroinvertebrates or fishes (e.g., reduced shading)?

In light of these questions and the broader goals outlined above, this protocol will address the following specific measurable monitoring objectives:

1. Determine the status of riparian condition, as measured by greenline and channel cross-section wetland ratings (i.e., obligate wetland riparian plant species cover), effective ground cover, and greenline woody vegetation cover for selected wadeable stream reaches in BIHO, CIRO, JODA, NEPE, and WHMI.
2. Determine the direction and magnitude of change over time for obligate wetland riparian plant species cover, effective ground cover, and woody vegetation cover, in BIHO, CIRO, JODA, NEPE, and WHMI.
3. Determine the condition of riparian zones along selected wadeable UCBN stream reaches, relative to PIBO sample reaches in the same watershed.
4. Determine the status and trend in the cover of non-native invasive plant species (e.g., *Acroptilon repens*) found along UCBN streams, as estimated from PIBO sample reaches.

Study Area

John Day River- John Day Fossil Beds National Monument (JODA), Sheep Rock Unit

The Sheep Rock unit of JODA is in the Upper John Day Watershed, Hydrologic Unit 17070201 (United States Geologic Survey [USGS]), in Grant County, Oregon (Figures 1 and 2). The drainage area for the John Day River above the park is approximately 4,351 square km (1,680 square miles) and consists of several land cover types (NPS 1997). According to Bell and Hinson 2010, Sheep Rock's watersheds are dominated by the following land cover types: big sagebrush-bluebunch wheatgrass (*Aretimisia tridentate, Pseudoroegneria spicata*) (36.59%), Wyoming big sagebrush (*Aretimisia tridentata* spp. *wyomingensis*) (13.63%), and has less than 3% of the watersheds in agriculture or developed lands. In addition, over 25% of the Sheep Rock watersheds are tree dominated vegetation, primarily ponderosa pine (*Pinus ponderosa*) and Douglas fir (*Pseudotsuga menziesii*)[Bell and Hinson 2010].

Designated beneficial uses for the John Day River and all its tributaries include: public and private domestic water supply, industrial water supply, irrigation, livestock watering, fish and aquatic life, wildlife and hunting, fishing, boating, water contact recreation, and aesthetic quality (OR DEQ 2010). Designated fish use is for salmon and trout rearing and migration (note: includes all salmon species, steelhead, rainbow and cutthroat trout. The designated salmon and steelhead spawning use is from January 1 – May 15(OR DEQ 2010)).

Five sample sites/reaches were established starting from the downstream park boundary. Both stream channel characteristics and riparian condition were evaluated at each site. The most upstream sample site ended just upstream of the Cant ranch house (Figure3). Note that stream channel characteristics and riparian condition were not evaluated at sample site #3078, it was sampled exclusively for benthic macroinvertebrates.

Figure 1. John Day River looking upstream towards Picture Gorge.

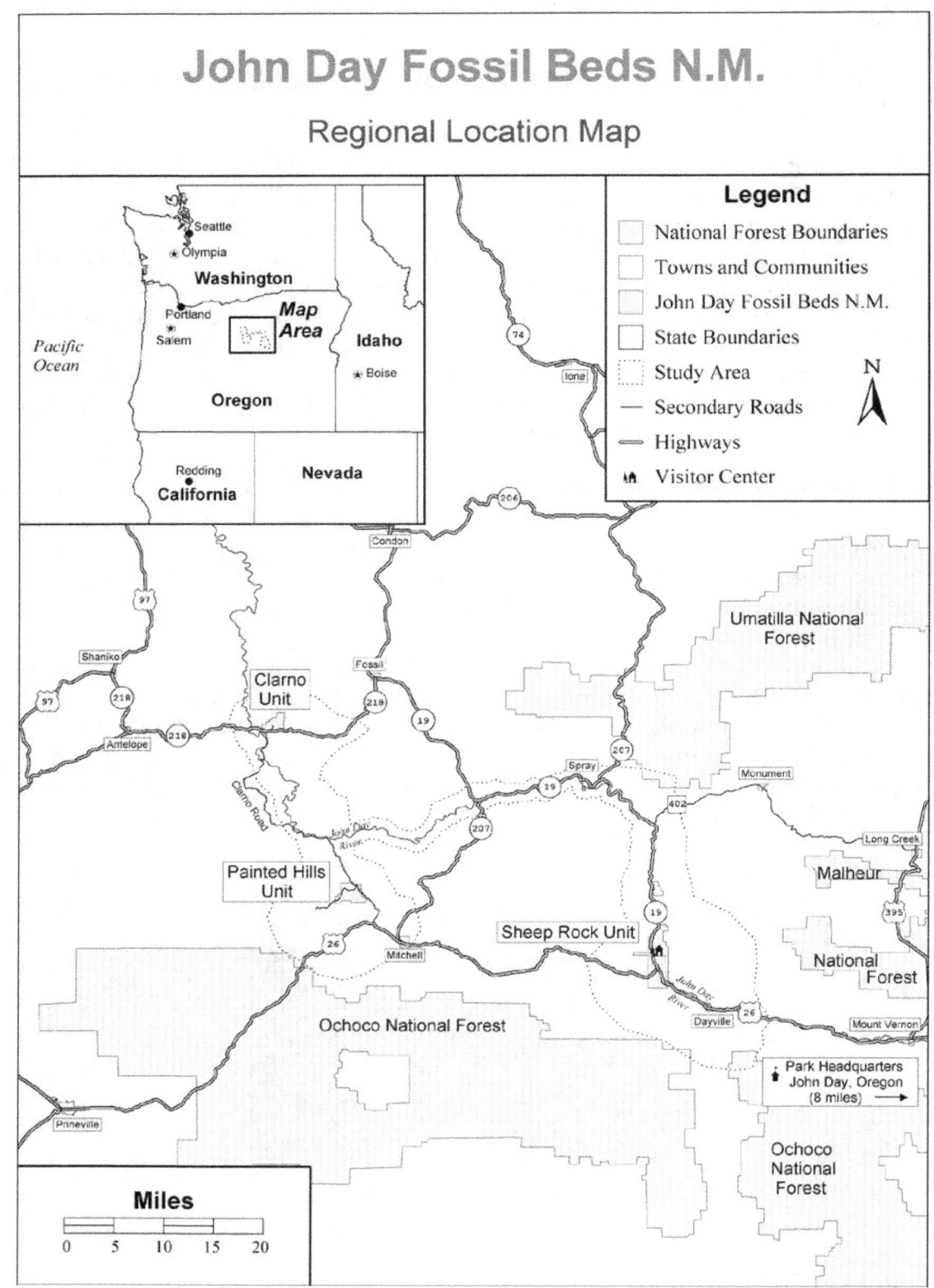

Figure 2. John Day Fossil Beds National Monument regional map (NPS 1997).

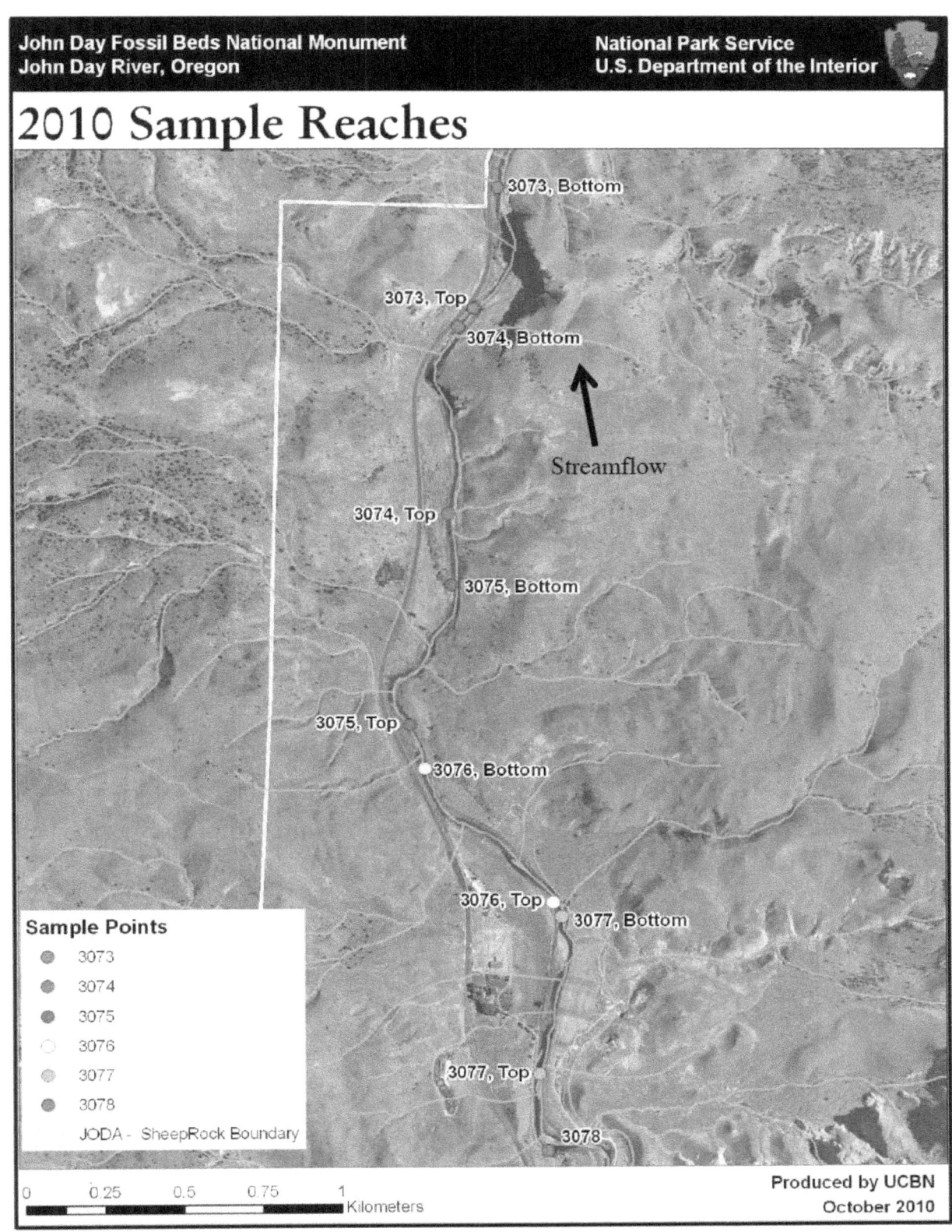

Figure 3. Top and bottom of stream channel characteristic and riparian condition monitoring sites in the John Day River 2010.

Methods

Data from the 2010 field sampling effort was collected following methods detailed in the UCBN stream channel characteristics and riparian condition monitoring protocols (Starkey et al. 2011, Starkey et al. 2010). The UCBN's protocols mirror existing monitoring protocols developed by the United States Forest Service (USFS) PACFISH/INFISH Effectiveness Monitoring (PIBO-EM) Program (Heitke et al. 2009, Leary and Ebertowski 2010). In addition to the use of existing protocols, the UCBN has formed an interagency agreement with the USFS such that the PIBO program collects the data necessary to complete stream channel and riparian monitoring in the UCBN. The use of existing tested protocols and trained field crew promotes data quality and integration of data from the UCBN with data collected throughout the region. This approach will provide a unique opportunity to examine park stream channel and riparian resources relative to regional status and trends. A more detailed description of the PIBO programs purpose and approach to monitoring can be found in Kershner et al. (2004b) and Henderson et al. (2005).

To achieve the measurable objectives, the PIBO program established 5-sites as described below and sampled the John Day River in August, during base flow conditions.

Data Collection

All data collection was conducted by the USFS PIBO Program in accordance with the PIBO Sampling Protocol for Stream Channel Attributes (Heitke et al. 2009) and Sampling Protocol for Vegetation Parameters (Leary and Ebertowski 2010). These protocols are available from the PIBO website (http://www.fs.fed.us/biology/fishecology/emp/ Accessed 20 January 2010).

Locating Stream Channel, Riparian and Additional Macroinvertebrate Sample Reaches

Sample reach selection differed slightly from standard PIBO methods due to the restriction placed on the sampling design by park boundaries. Typically sample reach locations are chosen by moving upstream from the bottom of a randomly selected 6th field HUC until a pool tail is reached. As a result of this boundary restriction, the location of the first sample reach was determined by the field crew moving upstream from the park boundary until the first pool tail was identified. Subsequent sample reaches within the park were determined by moving upstream from a previous sample reach until another pool tail was identified. Pools are clearly defined in the "Pools" section of the PIBO Sampling Protocol for Stream Channel Attributes (Heitke, et al. 2009). It is important to note that stream channel and riparian sample reaches are co-located. The additional benthic macroinvertebrate sample location was identified in the same manner and fell above the most upstream stream channel sample reach. The top and bottom of each sample reach were permanently marked using a 1 inch by 3 inch piece of aluminum with PIBO EM scratched into them (Figure 4). The top of each reach was labeled with the site number and TR for Top Reach and the bottom of each reach with the site number and BR for Bottom Reach. In subsequent years, during revisits, field crews will navigate back to the same sample reach using a reach description (Appendix D), photographs (Appendix E), topographic map and UTM coordinates.

Figure 4. Marker at the bottom of JODA reach #3074, August 2010.

Results

Note that this report is a data series report and intended as a release of basic data sets and data summaries. Care has been taken to assure accuracy of raw data values, but thorough analysis and interpretation of the data has not been completed. More extensive analysis and discussion of stream channel characteristics and riparian condition will occur as part of the trend analysis, which will be available after 3 years of monitoring data become available.

Stream Channel Characteristics/Riparian Condition

The status of individual stream channel parameters is shown in Table 1. Greenline wetland ratings and status of individual riparian attributes are shown in Table 2. A summary of weeds encountered during the riparian assessment is given in Table 3. Descriptions of each parameter are given in Appendix C.

Data collected in 2011 represents the first stream channel and riparian assessment on the John Day River within JODA. Therefore, all data should be considered baseline information to which future assessments can be compared. The next assessment will occur in 2013, with a preliminary assessment of trend in 2016.

Table 1. Vital sign summary table for stream channel characteristics in the John Day River within JODA, 2010.

John Day River Stream Channel Characteristics Summary 2010

Parameter (Units)	Abbreviation	Site ID/Reach ID					Mean	Standard Deviation
		3073/5871	3074/5872	3075/5873	3076/5874	3077/5875		
Average bankfull width from transects (m)	Bf	23.67	28.64	23.31	25.89	26.22	25.55	2.16
Length of the reach (m)	RchLen	432	629	577	626	532	559.20	81.50
Gradient of stream reach (%)	Grad	0.72	0.628	0.282	0.179	0.256	0.41	0.24
Sinuosity of stream reach (ratio)	Sin	1.081	1.031	1.201	1.052	1.029	1.08	0.07
Residual pool depth (m)	Pooldp	1.63	0.73	0.68	1.22	1.47	1.15	0.43
Percent pools (%)	PoolPct	77.89	34.85	64.84	68.96	54.29	60.17	16.50
Number of pools per kilometer.(# / km)	PoolFrq	6.94	7.95	8.67	7.99	3.76	7.06	1.95
Bankfull width to depth ratio at transects (ratio)	WDTrans	24.63	38.14	31.79	32.09	37.92	32.91	5.54
Wetted width to depth ratio at transects (ratio)	WDwetTrans	38.4	60.99	49.67	63.19	98.28	62.11	22.51
Diameter of the 50th percentile streambed particle (m)	D50	0.2	0.1	0.05	0.04	0.04	0.09	0.07
Percent pool tail fines < 2mm (%)	PIFn2	6.44	8.67	5.87	13.33	18.33	10.53	5.26
Percent pool tail fines < 6mm (%)	PIFn6	12.22	17.17	13.73	22.83	23	17.79	5.01
Average bank angle (degrees)	BnkAngl	136	145	140	135	124	136.00	7.78
Percent stable banks (covered stable, false bank, and uncovered stable). (%)	Stab	97.73	100	94.87	92	94.59	95.84	3.09
Percent of bank angles < 90 (%)°	UnCutPct	15.91	8	10.53	10	21.62	13.21	5.54
Large wood frequency (pieces / km)	LWfreq	11.6	0	0	4.8	9.4	5.16	5.31
Large wood volume (m³ / km)	LWvol	1.8	0	0	1.11	2.3	1.04	1.04

Table 2. Vital sign summary table for riparian condition along the John Day River within JODA, 2010.

John Day River Riparian Condition Summary 2010

Parameter (Units)	Abbreviation	Site ID/Reach ID					Mean	Standard Deviation
		3073/5871	3074/5872	3075/5873	3076/5874	3077/5875		
Greenline total cover (%)	GLtotalcv	54.1	64.4	60.4	78.1	69.5	65.30	9.11
Greenline relative alien cover (%)	GLrac	0	0	3.5	0	0.3	0.76	1.54
Greenline relative cover nativity unknown (%)	GLunid	1.7	0	0	0	0	0.34	0.76
Cross-section total cover (%)	XStotalcv	21.8	45.7	70.5	70.2	58.7	53.38	20.38
Cross-section relative alien cover (%)	XSrac	16	9.4	0.5	11.5	15	10.48	6.18
Cross-section relative cover nativity unknown (%)	XSunid	0	0	0	0	0	0.00	0.00
Reach native cover (%)	RchNtvcv	39.1	55.8	63	72.1	61.2	58.24	12.20
Reach alien cover (%)	RchAlncv	1.4	1.6	1.4	3	3.8	2.24	1.10
Reach cover nativity unknown (%)	RchUnidcv	0.5	0	0	0	0	0.10	0.22
Reach total cover (%)	RchTotalcv	41	57.4	64.4	75.2	65	60.60	12.66
Effective ground cover (%)	EGC	84.2	92	81.7	96.5	97.3	90.34	7.10
Richness native (# native species)	Sntv	9	14	12	13	11	11.80	1.92
Richness alien (# non-native species)	Saln	1	1	2	4	3	2.20	1.30
Richness nativity unknown (# unknown-nativity)	Sunid	1	0	0	0	0	0.20	0.45
Richness total (# of species)	Stotal	11	15	14	17	15	14.40	2.19
Greenline woody cover (%)	GLwoodycv	16.2	2.1	9	7.4	14.2	9.78	5.61
Greenline wetland rating (unitless)	GLwetrat	83	78.4	77.8	79.1	76.3	78.92	2.50
Cross-section wetland rating (unitless)	XSwetrat	66.3	67.7	81.3	68.9	53.6	67.56	9.84

Table 3. Vital sign summary table for weeds in riparian areas along the John Day River within JODA, 2010. Note that species listed as weeds are listed as noxious weeds in the INVADERS Database System http://invader.dbs.umt.edu (Rice 2011).

John Day River Weeds Summary 2010

Site ID	Reach ID	Plant Species	Common Name	Greenline weed cover (%)	Cross-section weed cover (%)
3073	5871	*Phalaris arundinacea*	reed canarygrass	6.5	0.3
3073	5871	*Equisetum arvense*	field horsetail	0.2	0
3074	5872	*Phalaris arundinacea*	reed canarygrass	5.2	14.2
3074	5872	*Equisetum arvense*	field horsetail	0.6	0
3074	5872	*Elymus repens*	quackgrass	0	4.3
3075	5873	*Phalaris arundinacea*	reed canarygrass	13.6	17.6
3075	5873	*Equisetum arvense*	field horsetail	2.2	0
3076	5874	*Phalaris arundinacea*	reed canarygrass	23.8	36.8
3076	5874	*Linaria dalmatica*	Dalmatian toadflax	0	0.3
3076	5874	*Equisetum arvense*	field horsetail	0.6	0
3076	5874	*Elymus repens*	quackgrass	0	2.9
3077	5875	*Phalaris arundinacea*	reed canarygrass	24.8	14.6
3077	5875	*Equisetum arvense*	field horsetail	1.4	0.7

Literature Cited

Bell, J. and D. Hinson. 2010. Natural resource condition assessment: John Day Fossil Beds National Monument. Natural Resource Report NPS/UCBN/NRR—2010/174. National Park Service, Fort Collins, CO.

Garrett, L. K., T. J. Rodhouse, G. H. Dicus, C. C. Caudill, and M. R. Shardlow. 2007. Vitals Signs Monitoring Plan, Upper Columbia Basin Network. Natural Resource Report NPS/PWR/UCBN/NRR—2007/002. National Park Service, Fort Collins, CO.

Heitke, J D., E. K. Archer, and B. B. Roper. 2009. Effectiveness monitoring for streams and riparian areas: sampling protocol for stream channel attributes. PACFISH/INFISH-Biological Opinion Effectiveness Monitoring Program (PIBO-EM). Logan, UT. (http://www.fs.fed.us/biology/fishecology/emp). Accessed 18 January 2010.

Leary, R. J., and P. Ebertowski. 2010. Effectiveness monitoring for streams and riparian areas: sampling protocol for vegetation parameters. PACFISH/INFISH- Biological Opinion Effectiveness Monitoring Program (PIBO-EM). Logan, UT. (Unpublished paper at: http://www.fs.fed.us/biology/fishecology/emp). Accessed on 31 May 2010.

National Park Service (NPS) 1997. Baseline water quality data inventory and analysis: John Day Fossil Beds National Monument. NPS/NRWRD/NRTR-97/112. Fort Collins, CO.

National Park Service (NPS). 1999. Natural resource challenge: the National Park Service's action plan for preserving natural resources. US Department of the Interior National Park Service, Washington D.C. (http://www.nature.nps.gov/challenge/challengedoc/index.htm). Accessed 18 February 2010.

Oregon Department of Environmental Quality (OR DEQ). 2010. John Day River basin total maximum daily load (TMDL) and water quality management plan (WQMP). DEQ 10-WQ-025. Oregon Department of Environmental Quality. Portland, OR.

Rice, P. M. 2011. INVADERS Database System. Division of Biological Sciences, University of Montana, Missoula, MT. (http://invader.dbs.umt.edu). Accessed on 16 May 2011.

Starkey, E. N. 2011. Upper Columbia Basin Network integrated water quality annual report 2010: John Day Fossil Beds National Monument (JODA). Natural Resource Technical Report NPS/UCBN/NRTR—2011/XXX. National Park Service, Fort Collins, CO.

Starkey, E. N., T. J. Rodhouse, G. H. Dicus, L. K. Garrett, K. M. Irvine, and E. K. Archer. 2011. Upper Columbia Basin Network stream channel characteristics monitoring protocol: Narrative version 1.0. Natural Resource Report NPS/UCBN/NRR—2011/340. National Park Service, Fort Collins, CO. (http://science.nature.nps.gov/im/units/ucbn/reports/index.cfm#IWQ Mon). Accessed 04 April 2011.

Starkey, E. N., T. J. Rodhouse, G. H. Dicus, L. K. Garrett, K. M. Irvine, and E. K. Archer. 2010. Upper Columbia Basin Network riparian condition monitoring protocol: Narrative version 1.0. Natural Resource Report NPS/UCBN/NRR—2010/00xxx. National Park Service, Fort Collins, CO.

Appendix A. Hydrologic Unit Code Boundaries, JODA- Sheep Rock Unit

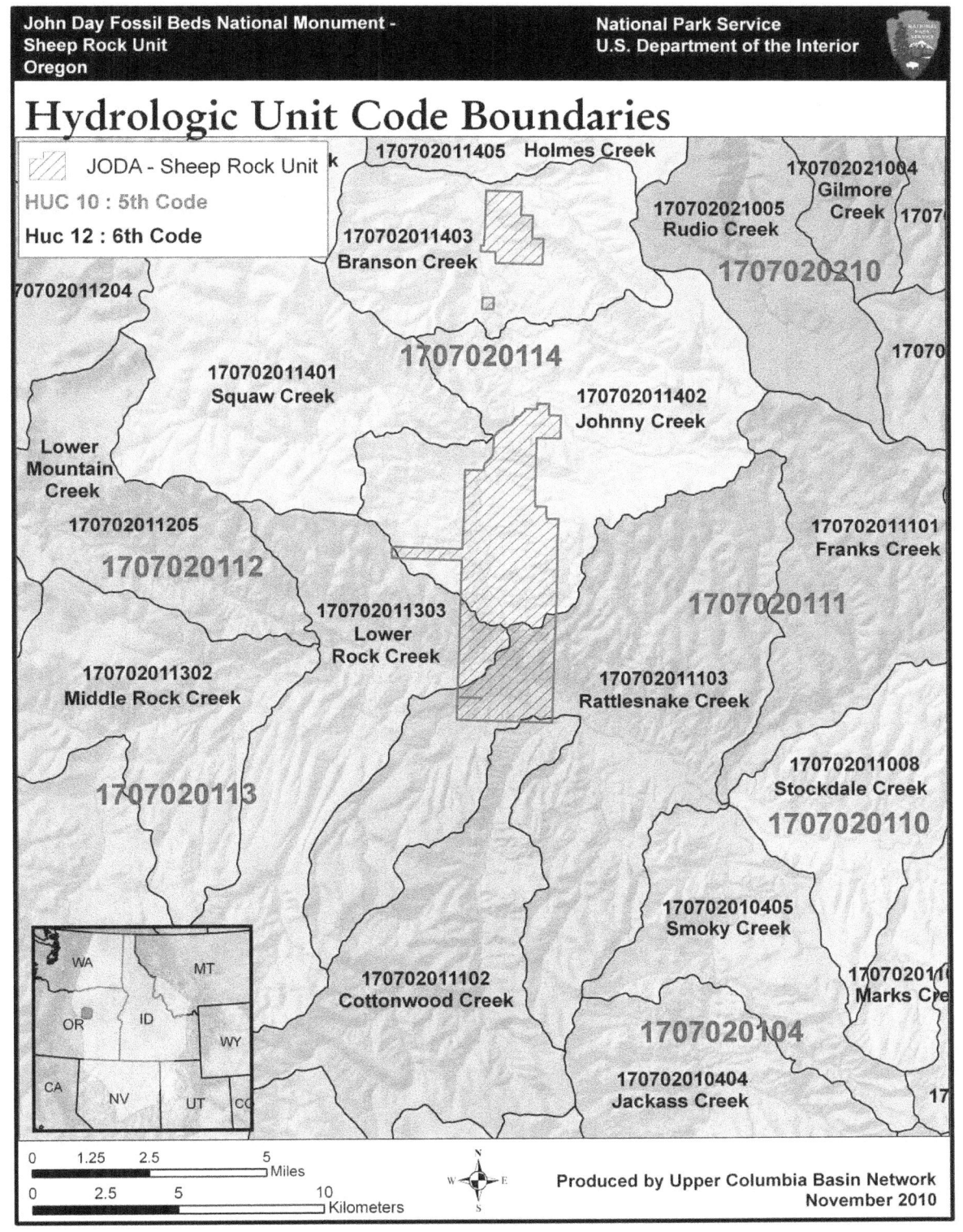

Appendix B. Stream Channel Monitoring Locations, JODA 2010

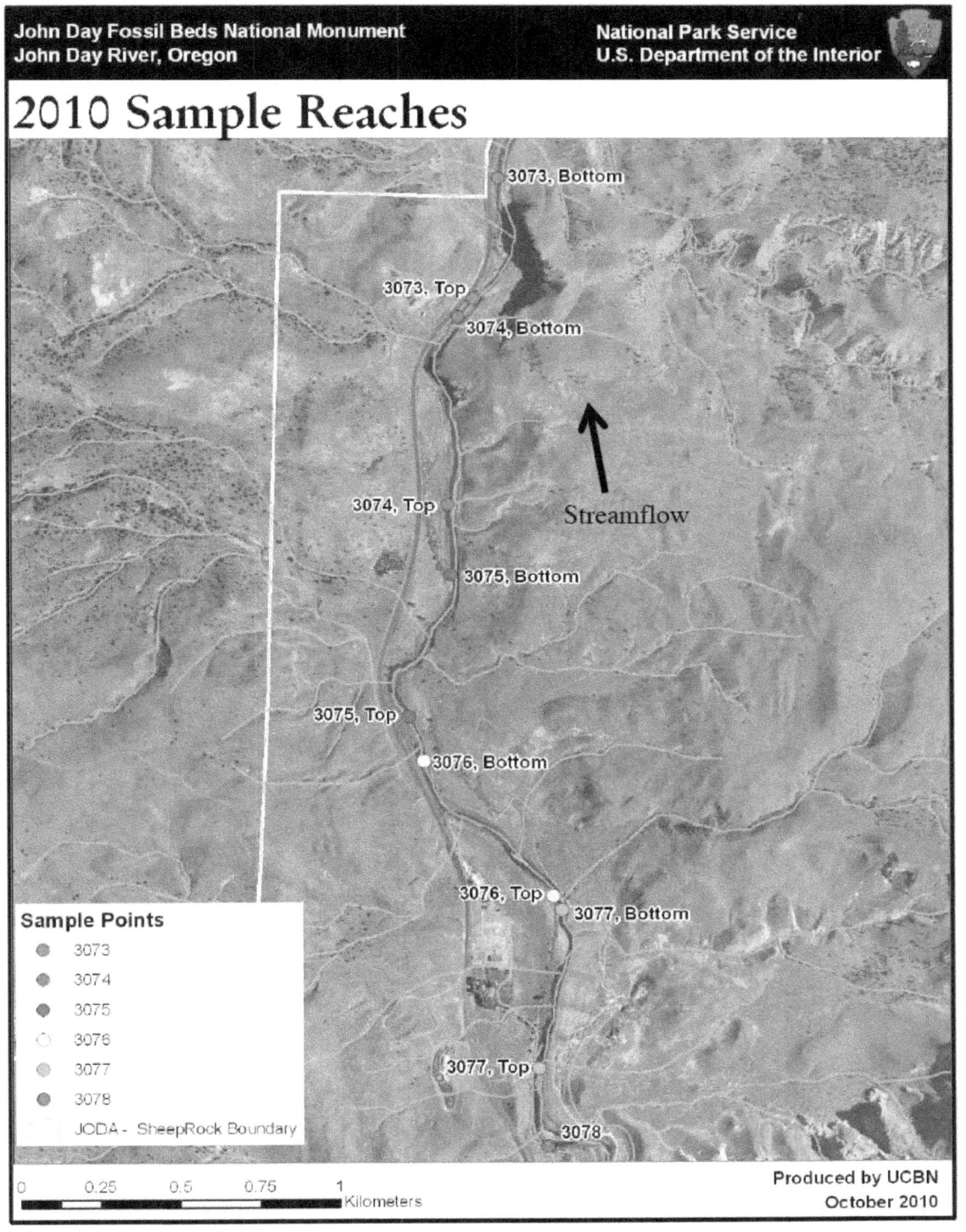

Appendix C. Parameter Descriptions for Riparian, Stream Channel and Weed Monitoring

The descriptions of each parameter have been provided by PIBO as part of the data summaries for stream channel and riparian monitoring.

Riparian Condition

Cross-section relative alien cover: The proportion of cross-section plant cover coming from non-native species. Calculated as species cover of non-natives divided by total species cover, and multiplied by 100. (Magee et al. 2008.)

Cross-section relative cover nativity unknown: The relative cross-section plant cover of species with nativity status unknown. Calculated as cover of species with nativity unknown divided by total species cover, and multiplied by 100. NOTE: This value is relativized, and not comparable to other reported (actual) cover values.

Cross-section total cover: Total plant cover for riparian cross-section. Because cover is estimated for two layers (1m and below, above 1m) total species cover can be a maximum of 200 percent.

Cross-section wetland rating: A measure of the abundance of wetland species in the riparian area. A wetland rating of 100 indicating all obligate wetland species and 1 being all upland species. The rating is calculated for each reach by summing the product of the relative cover of each species for which a wetland indicator status can be determined and a value corresponding to the species' wetland indicator status (1=upland, 25= facultative upland, 50=facultative, 75=facultative wet, 100=obligate wetland. Coles-Ritchie et al. 2007).The cross-section sample area was a fixed area, 3 to 9.5 m from the greenline.

Effective ground cover: The percent of the riparian area (not including the greenline) with effective ground cover. The cross-section average percent cover of bare soil is subtracted from 100 to calculate effective ground cover. Live vegetation within 1 m of the ground, litter, and rocks greater than 2.5 cm are considered effective ground cover. Prior to 2009, data for calculating effective ground cover were collected at the four corners of the quadrat, rather than for the entire quadrat. Because of the different methods, 2009 and 2010 effective ground cover data are not comparable to earlier years.

Greenline relative alien cover: The proportion of greenline plant cover coming from non-native species. Calculated as species cover of non-natives divided by total species cover, and multiplied by 100. (Magee et al. 2008.)

Greenline relative cover nativity unknown: The relative greenline plant cover of species with nativity status unknown. Calculated as cover of species with nativity unknown divided by total species cover, and multiplied by 100. NOTE: This value is relativized, and not comparable to other reported (actual) cover values.

Appendix C. Parameter Descriptions for Riparian, Stream Channel and Weed Monitoring (continued)

Greenline total cover: Total plant cover for greenline. Because cover is estimated for two layers (1m and below, above 1m) total species cover can be a maximum of 200 percent.

Greenline wetland rating: A measure of the abundance of wetland species along the streambank. A wetland rating of 100 indicating all obligate wetland species and 1 being all upland species. The rating is calculated for each reach by summing the product of the relative cover of each species for which a wetland indicator status can be determined and a value corresponding to the species' wetland indicator status (1=upland, 25= facultative upland, 50=facultative, 75=facultative wet, 100=obligate wetland. Coles-Ritchie et al. 2007).

Greenline woody cover: The sum of the percent cover of woody species along the greenline. These could be any woody species, such as willows, pines, or currants. Greenline woody cover can be up to 200% because cover estimates are a combination of two layers.

Reach alien cover: Non-native species cover for combined greenline and cross-section. Because cover is estimated for two layers (1m and below, above 1m) total species cover can be a maximum of 200 percent.

Reach cover nativity unknown: Cover of species with nativity status unknown for combined greenline and cross-section. Because cover is estimated for two layers (1m and below, above 1m) total species cover can be a maximum of 200 percent.

Reach native cover: Native species cover for combined greenline and cross-section. Because cover is estimated for two layers (1m and below, above 1m) total species cover can be a maximum of 200 percent.

Reach total cover: Total species cover for combined greenline and cross-section. Because cover is estimated for two layers (1m and below, above 1m) total species cover can be a maximum of 200 percent.

Richness alien: Number of non-native species for combined greenline and cross-section.

Richness native: Number of native species for combined greenline and cross-section.

Richness nativity unknown: Number of species with nativity status unknown for combined greenline and cross-section.

Richness total: Total number of species for combined greenline and cross-section.

Appendix C. Parameter Descriptions for Riparian, Stream Channel and Weed Monitoring (continued)

Stream Channel Characteristics

Average bankfull width from transects: Bankfull widths are measured at each transect. This is the average of the 21-25 transects typically measured at each reach.

Bank angle: Average of all bank angle measurements. Bank angles <45 degrees are summarized as 45 degrees.

Bankfull width-to-depth ratio at riffles: 2001-2008. Average of the bankfull width-to-depth ratios from four channel cross-sections. Cross-sections were measured at the widest location (bankfull width) in the first 4 riffles within straight stream segments. Each ratio was calculated as bankfull width divided by the bankfull depth. Bankfull depth was calculated as the total bankfull area divided by the bankfull width. Some reaches had <4 cross sections if suitable locations could not be found.

Bankfull width-to-depth ratio at transects: ≥ 2009. Average of the bankfull width-to-depth ratio from 10 cross sections at / near even numbered transects 2-20. If there were <6 suitable measurements, or water surface was not level (>0.03cm variance between banks) no value is reported. Each ratio was calculated as bankfull width divided by the bankfull depth. Bankfull depth was calculated as the total bankfull area divided by the bankfull width.

Diameter of the 50th percentile streambed particle: Diameter of the 50th percentile particles. Typically more than 100 particles measured per reach. Bedrock and bank particles are measured but later excluded from the calculation. Sampling methods have changed. Presently, five particles are collected along each transect (2004-present). From 1998-2003, measured particles were gathered within riffle habitat.

Gradient of stream reach: The difference between the elevation of the water surface at the bottom of the reach and the elevation of the water surface at the top of the reach divided by the reach length (measured along the thalweg). The result is multiplied by 100 to express the value as a percent.

Large wood frequency: Number of category 1 large wood pieces measured within the reach and then standardized to per kilometer. Category 1 criteria: length ≥1m, diameter ≥0.1m, some portion must be within the bankfull channel and below the bankfull elevation.

Large wood volume: Volume of category 1 large wood pieces measured within the reach and then standardized to per kilometer. Category 1 criteria: length ≥1m, diameter ≥0.1m, some portion must be within the bankfull channel and below the bankfull elevation.

Length of sampling reach: Length of sampling reach measured along the thalweg

Appendix C. Parameter Descriptions for Riparian, Stream Channel and Weed Monitoring (continued)

Number of pools per kilometer: Number of pools within the sampled reach standardized to pools per kilometer.

Percent of bank angles < 90°: Number of transect locations with bank angles <90 degrees divided by the total number of transect bank measurements. The result is multiplied by 100 to express the value as a percent.

Percent pool tail fines: Quantified using a 0.36m x 0.36m grid with 50 intersections. The grid is placed at 3 locations along each pool tail. The percentage of particles <2mm and <6mm is calculated for each grid, averaged for each pool, then averaged for all pools within the reach.

Percent pools: Sum of all qualifying pool lengths divided by the reach length. The result is multiplied by 100 to express the value as a percent.

Percent stable banks: The number of covered stable, uncovered stable, and false bank measurements divided by the total number of measurements. The result is multiplied by 100 to express the value as a percent.

Residual pool depth: Average of the residual pool depth values for all pools in a reach. Residual pool depth is calculated for each qualifying pool by subtracting the pool tail depth from the max depth.

Sinuosity of stream reach: Reach length measured along the thalweg divided by the straight valley length from the bottom of the reach to the top of the reach. Straight valley length is presently determined using UTM coordinates, but was measured using a tape measure <2009.

Wetted width-to-depth ratio at riffles: 2001-2008. Average ratio of wetted width-to-depth ratio from four channel cross-sections. Cross-sections were measured at the widest location (bankfull width) in the first 4 riffles within straight stream segments. Each ratio was calculated as wetted width divided by the wetted depth. Wetted depth was calculated as the total wetted area divided by the wetted width. Some reaches had <4 cross sections if suitable locations could not be found.

Wetted width-to-depth ratio at transects: ≥ 2009. Average of the wetted width-to-depth ratio from 10 cross sections at / near even numbered transects 2-20. If there were <6 suitable measurements, or water surface was not level (>0.03cm variance between banks) no value is reported. Each ratio was calculated as wetted width divided by the wetted depth. Wetted depth was calculated as the total wetted area divided by the wetted width.

Appendix C. Parameter Descriptions for Riparian, Stream Channel and Weed Monitoring (continued)

Weeds

Common name: Common name of plant species

Cross-section weed cover (%): The percent cover of the species in the riparian cross-section, 3 to 9.5 m from the greenline, that is on a combined list of noxious weeds, based on Rice (2007), for any of five states (ID, MT, NV, OR, WA) in the study area.

Greenline weed cover (%): The percent cover along the greenline of the species that is on a combined list of noxious weeds, based on Rice (2007), for any of five states (ID, MT, NV, OR, WA) in the study area.

Plant species: Scientific name of plant species

Appendix D. Site Information Sheets, JODA 2010

Site Information Sheet

SiteID	SiteName	Stream	Forest	District
3073	523-01-1	John Day		

Rand Start:	*Length:*	*Width Cat:* 20	*Brush Factor:* 1	*Wood Factor:* 1

Last Sample Date: 8/17/2010

UTM Coordinates:

UTM Zone:	*Bottom East :*	*Bottom North :*
	Top East :	*Top North :*

Driving Directions: *DriveTime:* 00:20   *DriveFrom:* Dayville

From the Dayvile Merc, drive west on Hwy 26 for 6.7 mi. Turn Right/North on Hwy 19 and Reset Odometer (RO). Drive 3.6 mi. and park at a pullout on the right near two large junipers, across the road from the "Goose Rock" sign (the more northern one).

Hiking Directions: *Hike Time:* 00:02   *Hike Distance:* 35 meters

Walk down the slope to th river and head down stream to the BR.

Camping Options:

Lone Pine Camp Ground. Continue north on Hwy 19 for ~15 mi. then turn right (east) on Hwy 402. Drive ~1.6 mi. The camp ground is on the right.

Additional Comments:

This is a NPS site. Have the NPS sampling permit with you in the truck when doing this site. Call ahead to the Park Service to let them know you will be sampling in the area.

Site Marker Info:

Bottom of Reach	*UTM East:* 290072	*UTM North:* 1939336
Description: ON USFS SIGN ON ROADNEAR RL	*Bearing:* 32	*Distance to Bottom:* 35

Top of Reach	*UTM East:* 290005	*UTM North:* 4938974
Description: ON DOWNED LOG ON RL	*Bearing:* 80	*Distance to Top:* 10

Site Information Sheet

SiteID	SiteName	Stream	Forest	District
3073	523-01-I	John Day		

Site Map:

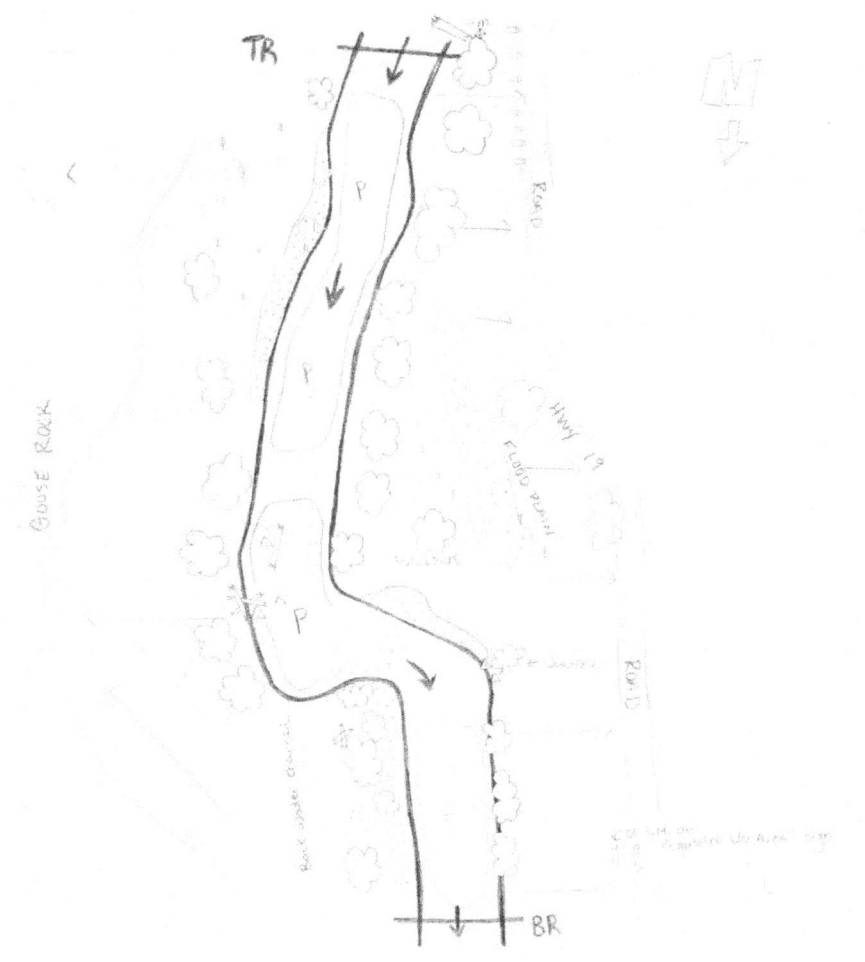

Site Information Sheet

SiteID	SiteName	Stream	Forest	District
3074	523-02-1	John Day		

Rand Start:	**Length:**	**Width Cat:** 26	**Brush Factor:** 1	**Wood Factor:** 1

Last Sample Date: 8/18/2010

UTM Coordinates:

UTM Zone:	Bottom East :	Bottom North :
	Top East :	Top North :

Driving Directions: **DriveTime:** 00:20   **DriveFrom:** Dayville

From the Dayvile Merc, drive west on Hwy 26 for 6.7 mi. Turn Right/North on Hwy 19 and Reset Odometer (RO). Drive 3.2 mi. and park at a pullout on the Left, just before the guard rail starts on the Right.

Hiking Directions: **Hike Time:** 00:05   **Hike Distance:** 100 meters

Walk across the road and down the slope to the BR.

Camping Options:

Lone Pine Camp Ground. Continue north on Hwy 19 for ~15 mi. then turn right (east) on Hwy 402. Drive ~1.6 mi. The camp ground is on the right.

Additional Comments:

This is a NPS site. Have the NPS sampling permit with you in the truck when doing this site. Call ahead to the Park Service to let them know you will be sampling in the area.

Site Marker Info:

Bottom of Reach	**UTM East:** 289947	**UTM North:** 4938922
Description:	**Bearing:** 113	**Distance to Bottom:** 20

INLINE WITH BR WOOD POST OF ROAD GUARD RAIL FACING STREAM

Top of Reach	**UTM East:** 289896	**UTM North:** 4938306
Description:	**Bearing:** 70	**Distance to Top:** 50

FALLEN TREE BETWEEN ROAD AND RIVINLINE W\ TR

Site Information Sheet

SiteID	SiteName	Stream	Forest	District
3074	523-02-1	John Day		

Site Map:

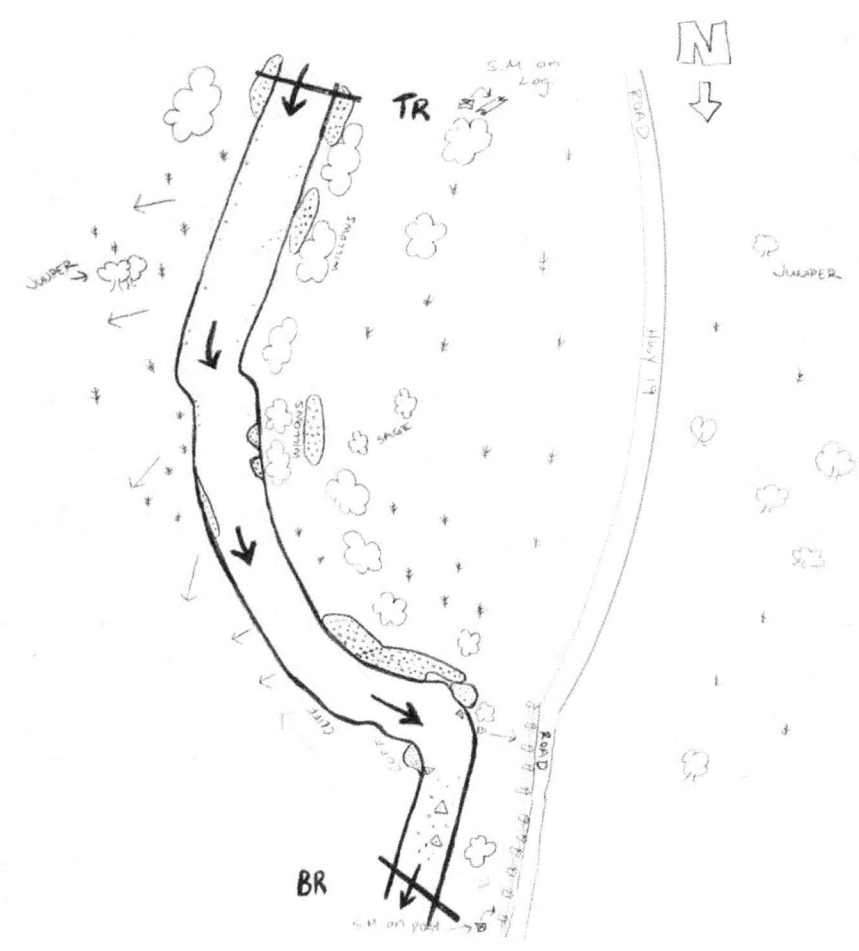

Site Information Sheet

SiteID	SiteName	Stream	Forest	District
3075	523-03-1	John Day		

Rand Start:	*Length:*	*Width Cat:* 26	*Brush Factor:* 1	*Wood Factor:* 1
Last Sample Date:	8/19/2010			

UTM Coordinates:

UTM Zone:	*Bottom East :*	*Bottom North :*
	Top East :	*Top North :*

Driving Directions: *DriveTime:* 00:20   *DriveFrom:* Dayville

From the Dayvile Merc, drive west on Hwy 26 for 6.7 mi. Turn Right/North on Hwy 19 and Reset Odometer (RO). Drive 2.8 mi. and park at in parking lot on the right, just after the guard rail.

Hiking Directions: *Hike Time:* 00:05   *Hike Distance:* 350 meters

Hike down stream to the BR.

Camping Options:

Lone Pine Camp Ground. Continue north on Hwy 19 for ~15 mi. then turn right (east) on Hwy 402. Drive ~1.6 mi. The camp ground is on the right.

Additional Comments:

This is a NPS site. Have the NPS sampling permit with you in the truck when doing this site. Call ahead to the Park Service to let them know you will be sampling in the area.

Site Marker Info:

Bottom of Reach	*UTM East:* 289920	*UTM North:* 4938072
Description:	*Bearing:* 74	*Distance to Bottom:* 15

ON DEAD WOOD ON BANKOF RL ADJACENT TO BR

Top of Reach	*UTM East:* 289872	*UTM North:* 4937590
Description:	*Bearing:* 274	*Distance to Top:* 50

LARGE JUNIPER ON BANK OF RR US FROM TR

Appendix D. Site Information Sheets, JODA 2010 (continued)

Site Information Sheet

SiteID	SiteName	Stream	Forest	District
3075	523-03-1	John Day		

Site Map:

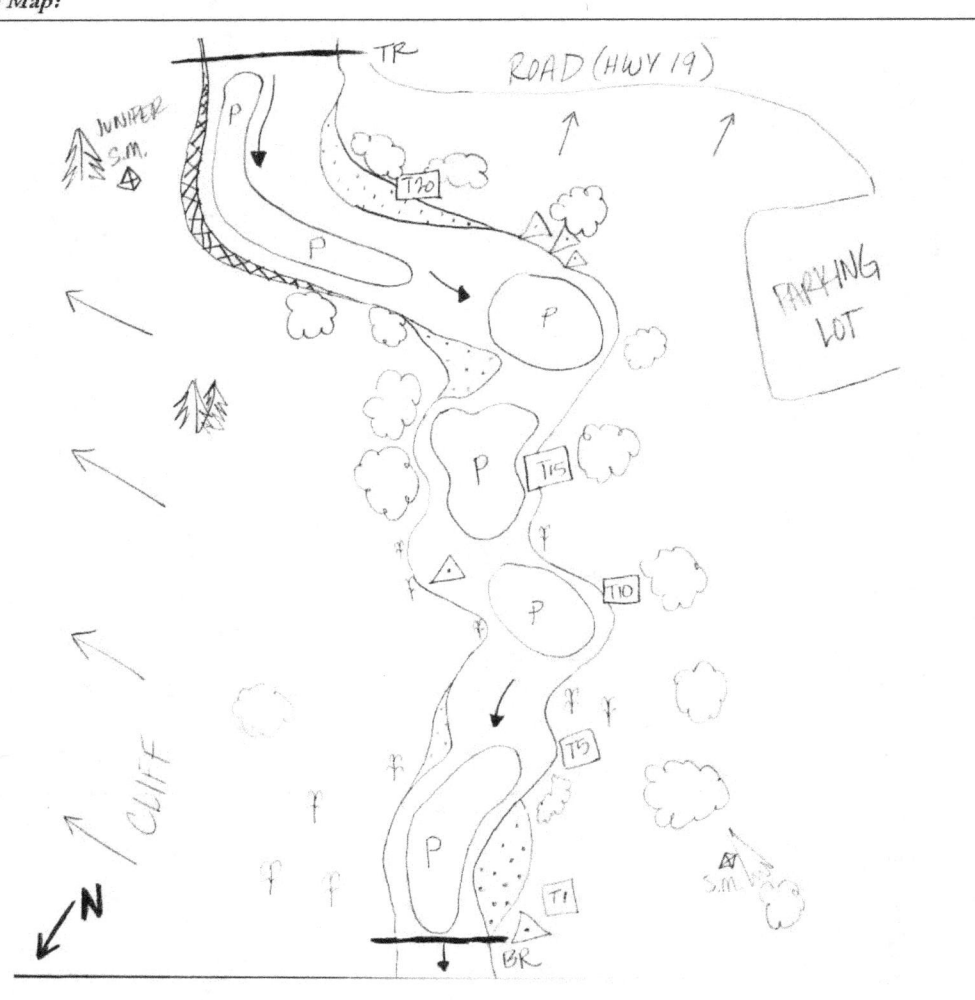

32

Site Information Sheet

SiteID	SiteName	Stream	Forest	District
3076	523-04-I	John Day		

Rand Start:	Length:	Width Cat: 26	Brush Factor: 1	Wood Factor: 1

Last Sample Date: 8/19/2010

UTM Coordinates:

UTM Zone:	Bottom East :	Bottom North :
	Top East :	Top North :

Driving Directions: Drive Time: 00:20   DriveFrom: Dayville

From the Dayvile Merc, drive west on Hwy 26 for 6.7 mi. Turn Right/North on Hwy 19 and Reset Odometer (RO). Drive 2.8 mi. and park at in parking lot on the right, just after the guard rail.

Hiking Directions: Hike Time: 00:05   Hike Distance: 200 meters

Hike upstream to the BR.

Camping Options:

Lone Pine Camp Ground. Continue north on Hwy 19 for ~15 mi. then turn right (east) on Hwy 402. Drive ~1.6 mi. The camp ground is on the right.

Additional Comments:

This is a NPS site. Have the NPS sampling permit with you in the truck when doing this site. Call ahead to the Park Service to let them know you will be sampling in the area.

Site Marker Info:

Bottom of Reach	UTM East: 289865	UTM North: 4937476
Description: ON THIRD US DECIDUOUS TREE	Bearing: 224	Distance to Bottom: 15

Top of Reach	UTM East: 290251	UTM North: 4936996
Description: ON POWER LINE POLE ON RL	Bearing: 22	Distance to Top: 30

Site Information Sheet

SiteID	SiteName	Stream	Forest	District
3076	523-04-I	John Day		

Site Map:

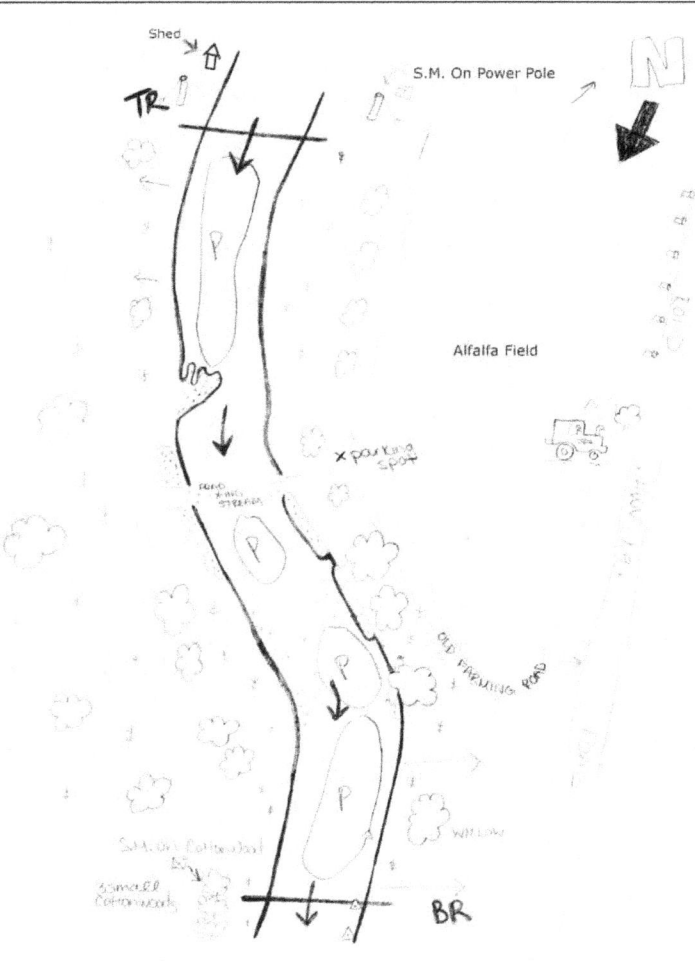

Site Information Sheet

SiteID	SiteName	Stream	Forest	District
3077	523-05-I	John Day		

Rand Start: *Length:*   *Width Cat:* 26   *Brush Factor:* 1   *Wood Factor:* 1

Last Sample Date: 8/20/2010

UTM Coordinates:

UTM Zone: *Bottom East :*   *Bottom North :*

    Top East :   *Top North :*

Driving Directions: *DriveTime:* 00:20   *DriveFrom:* Dayville

From the Dayvile Merc, drive west on Hwy 26 for 6.7 mi. Turn Right/North on Hwy 19 and Reset Odometer (RO). Drive 2.2 mi. and turn right into the Historic Cant Ranch Museum. Park in the lot.

Hiking Directions: *Hike Time:* 00:10   *Hike Distance:* 450 meters

Follow the John Day trail (paved or gravelled) around the alfalfa field to the Asiatic Elm tree (end of trail) From there cut down to the river (about 20 meters). Walk down stream to the BR.

Camping Options:

Lone Pine Camp Ground. Continue north on Hwy 19 for ~15 mi. then turn right (east) on Hwy 402. Drive ~1.6 mi. The camp ground is on the right.

Additional Comments:

This is a NPS site. Have the NPS sampling permit with you in the truck when doing this site. Call ahead to the Park Service to let them know you will be sampling in the area.

Watch out for rattle snakes!

Site Marker Info:

Bottom of Reach   *UTM East:*   *UTM North:*

Description: *Bearing:* 310   *Distance to Bottom:* 30
POWERLINE POLE ON RL.

Top of Reach   *UTM East:* 290169   *UTM North:* 4936440

Description: *Bearing:* 210   *Distance to Top:* 50
LARGE TREE ON RL USOF TR

Appendix D. Site Information Sheets, JODA 2010 (continued)

Site Information Sheet

SiteID	SiteName	Stream	Forest	District
3077	523-05-I	John Day		

Site Map:

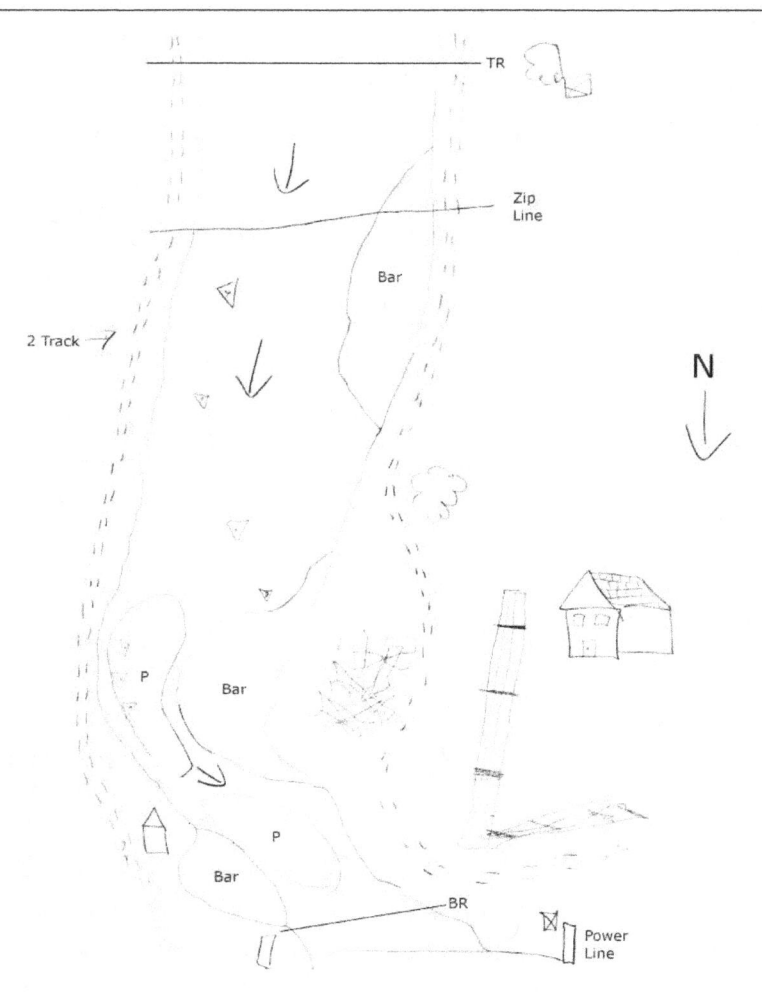

Site Information Sheet

SiteID	SiteName	Stream	Forest	District
3078	523-06-1	John Day		

Rand Start:	Length:	Width Cat: 26	Brush Factor: 1	Wood Factor: 1

Last Sample Date: 8/20/2010

UTM Coordinates:

UTM Zone:	Bottom East :	Bottom North :
	Top East :	Top North :

Driving Directions: DriveTime: 00:20   DriveFrom: Dayville

From the Dayvile Merc, drive west on Hwy 26 for 6.7 mi. Turn Right/North on Hwy 19 and Reset Odometer (RO). Drive 2.2 mi. and turn right into the Historic Cant Ranch Museum. Park in the lot.

Hiking Directions: Hike Time: 00:15   Hike Distance: 550 meters

From the Museum, take the two-track to the south east. Drop down the slope to the BR. The BR is at a large pool near a wide side channel.

Camping Options:

Lone Pine Camp Ground. Continue north on Hwy 19 for ~15 mi. then turn right (east) on Hwy 402. Drive ~1.6 mi. The camp ground is on the right.

Additional Comments:

This site is to collect Macro-invertebrates and conductivity & alkalinity ONLY!! Do not sample for any other data.

This is a NPS site. Have the NPS sampling permit with you in the truck when doing this site. Call ahead to the Park Service to let them know you will be sampling in the area.

Site Marker Info:

Bottom of Reach	UTM East: 290254	UTM North: 4936228
Description: DS of BF on RL LWD	Bearing: 250	Distance to Bottom: 20

Top of Reach	UTM East:	UTM North:
Description:	Bearing:	Distance to Top:

Appendix D. Site Information Sheets, JODA 2010 (continued)

Site Information Sheet

SiteID	SiteName	Stream	Forest	District
3078	523-06-I	John Day		

Site Map:

Appendix E. Stream Channel Monitoring Site Photos, JODA 2010

John Day, SiteID: 3073, SiteName: 523-01-I. Top of reach facing upstream. 8/17/2010

John Day, SiteID: 3073, SiteName: 523-01-I. Top of reach facing downstream. 8/17/2010

Appendix E. Stream Channel Monitoring Site Photos, JODA 2010 (continued)

John Day, SiteID: 3073, SiteName: 523-01-I. Reach Overview. 8/17/2010

John Day, SiteID: 3073, SiteName: 523-01-I. Misc Stream 4. 8/17/2010

Appendix E. Stream Channel Monitoring Site Photos, JODA 2010 (continued)

John Day, SiteID: 3073, SiteName: 523-01-I. Misc Stream 3. 8/17/2010

John Day, SiteID: 3073, SiteName: 523-01-I. Misc Stream 2. 8/17/2010

Appendix E. Stream Channel Monitoring Site Photos, JODA 2010 (continued)

John Day, SiteID: 3073, SiteName: 523-01-I. Misc Stream 1. 8/17/2010

John Day, SiteID: 3073, SiteName: 523-01-I. Marker Location Top Reach. ON DOWNED LOG ON RL10m to BR, bearing 80°. Site Marker UTMs East: 290005 North: 4938974 Zone: 11. 8/17/2010

Appendix E. Stream Channel Monitoring Site Photos, JODA 2010 (continued)

John Day, SiteID: 3073, SiteName: 523-01-I. Marker Location Bottom Reach. ON USFS SIGN ON ROADNEAR RL35m to BR, bearing 32°. Site Marker UTMs East: 290072 North: 4939336 Zone: 11. 8/17/2010

John Day, SiteID: 3073, SiteName: 523-01-I. Bottom of reach facing upstream. 8/17/2010

Appendix E. Stream Channel Monitoring Site Photos, JODA 2010 (continued)

John Day, SiteID: 3073, SiteName: 523-01-I. Bottom of reach facing downstream. 8/17/2010

Appendix E. Stream Channel Monitoring Site Photos, JODA 2010 (continued)

John Day, SiteID: 3074, SiteName: 523-02-I. Bottom of reach facing downstream. 8/18/2010

John Day, SiteID: 3074, SiteName: 523-02-I. Bottom of reach facing downstream. 8/18/2010

Appendix E. Stream Channel Monitoring Site Photos, JODA 2010 (continued)

John Day, SiteID: 3074, SiteName: 523-02-I. Top of reach facing upstream. 8/18/2010

John Day, SiteID: 3074, SiteName: 523-02-I. Reach Overview. 8/18/2010

Appendix E. Stream Channel Monitoring Site Photos, JODA 2010 (continued)

John Day, SiteID: 3074, SiteName: 523-02-I. Misc Stream 4. 8/18/2010

John Day, SiteID: 3074, SiteName: 523-02-I. Misc Stream 3. 8/18/2010

Appendix E. Stream Channel Monitoring Site Photos, JODA 2010 (continued)

John Day, SiteID: 3074, SiteName: 523-02-I. Misc Stream 2. 8/18/2010

John Day, SiteID: 3074, SiteName: 523-02-I. Misc Stream 1. 8/18/2010

Appendix E. Stream Channel Monitoring Site Photos, JODA 2010 (continued)

John Day, SiteID: 3074, SiteName: 523-02-I. Marker Location Top Reach. FALLEN TREE BETWEEN ROAD AND RIVINLINE W\ TR50m to BR, bearing 70°. Site Marker UTMs East: 289896 North: 4938306 Zone: 11. 8/18/2010

John Day, SiteID: 3074, SiteName: 523-02-I. Marker Location Bottom Reach. INLINE WITH BR WOOD POST OF ROAD GUARD RAIL FACING STREAM20m to BR, bearing 113°. Site Marker UTMs East: 289947 North: 4938922 Zone: 11. 8/18/2010

Appendix E. Stream Channel Monitoring Site Photos, JODA 2010 (continued)

John Day, SiteID: 3074, SiteName: 523-02-I. Bottom of reach facing upstream. 8/18/2010

Appendix E. Stream Channel Monitoring Site Photos, JODA 2010 (continued)

John Day, SiteID: 3075, SiteName: 523-03-I. Top of reach facing upstream. 8/19/2010

John Day, SiteID: 3075, SiteName: 523-03-I. Top of reach facing downstream. 8/19/2010

Appendix E. Stream Channel Monitoring Site Photos, JODA 2010 (continued)

John Day, SiteID: 3075, SiteName: 523-03-I. Reach Overview. 8/19/2010

John Day, SiteID: 3075, SiteName: 523-03-I. Misc Stream 3. 8/19/2010

Appendix E. Stream Channel Monitoring Site Photos, JODA 2010 (continued)

John Day, SiteID: 3075, SiteName: 523-03-I. Misc Stream 2. 8/19/2010

John Day, SiteID: 3075, SiteName: 523-03-I. Misc Stream 1. 8/19/2010

John Day, SiteID: 3075, SiteName: 523-03-I. Marker Location Top Reach. LARGE JUNIPER ON BANK OF RR US FROM TR50m to BR, bearing 274°. Site Marker UTMs East: 289872 North: 4937590 Zone: 11. 8/19/2010

John Day, SiteID: 3075, SiteName: 523-03-I. Marker Location Bottom Reach. ON DEAD WOOD ON BANKOF RL ADJACENT TO BR15m to BR, bearing 74°. Site Marker UTMs East: 289920 North: 4938072 Zone: 11. 8/19/2010

Appendix E. Stream Channel Monitoring Site Photos, JODA 2010 (continued)

John Day, SiteID: 3075, SiteName: 523-03-I. Bottom of reach facing upstream. 8/19/2010

John Day, SiteID: 3075, SiteName: 523-03-I. Bottom of reach facing downstream. 8/19/2010

Appendix E. Stream Channel Monitoring Site Photos, JODA 2010 (continued)

John Day, SiteID: 3076, SiteName: 523-04-I. Top of reach facing upstream. 8/20/2010

John Day, SiteID: 3076, SiteName: 523-04-I. Top of reach facing downstream. 8/20/2010

Appendix E. Stream Channel Monitoring Site Photos, JODA 2010 (continued)

John Day, SiteID: 3076, SiteName: 523-04-I. Reach Overview. 8/20/2010

John Day, SiteID: 3076, SiteName: 523-04-I. Misc Stream 3. 8/20/2010

Appendix E. Stream Channel Monitoring Site Photos, JODA 2010 (continued)

John Day, SiteID: 3076, SiteName: 523-04-I. Misc Stream 2. 8/20/2010

John Day, SiteID: 3076, SiteName: 523-04-I. Misc Stream 1. 8/20/2010

John Day, SiteID: 3076, SiteName: 523-04-I. Marker Location Top Reach. ON POWER LINE POLE ON RL30m to BR, bearing 22°. Site Marker UTMs East: 290251 North: 4936996 Zone: 11. 8/20/2010

John Day, SiteID: 3076, SiteName: 523-04-I. Marker Location Bottom Reach. ON THIRD US DECIDUOUS TREE15m to BR, bearing 224°. Site Marker UTMs East: 289865 North: 4937476 Zone: 11. 8/20/2010

Appendix E. Stream Channel Monitoring Site Photos, JODA 2010 (continued)

John Day, SiteID: 3076, SiteName: 523-04-I. Bottom of reach facing upstream. 8/20/2010

John Day, SiteID: 3076, SiteName: 523-04-I. Bottom of reach facing downstream. 8/20/2010

Appendix E. Stream Channel Monitoring Site Photos, JODA 2010 (continued)

John Day, SiteID: 3077, SiteName: 523-05-I. Top of reach facing upstream. 8/20/2010

John Day, SiteID: 3077, SiteName: 523-05-I. Top of reach facing downstream. 8/20/2010

Appendix E. Stream Channel Monitoring Site Photos, JODA 2010 (continued)

John Day, SiteID: 3077, SiteName: 523-05-I. Reach Overview. 8/20/2010

John Day, SiteID: 3077, SiteName: 523-05-I. Misc Stream 4. 8/20/2010

Appendix E. Stream Channel Monitoring Site Photos, JODA 2010 (continued)

John Day, SiteID: 3077, SiteName: 523-05-I. Misc Stream 3. 8/20/2010

John Day, SiteID: 3077, SiteName: 523-05-I. Misc Stream 2. 8/20/2010

Appendix E. Stream Channel Monitoring Site Photos, JODA 2010 (continued)

John Day, SiteID: 3077, SiteName: 523-05-I. Misc Stream 1. 8/20/2010

John Day, SiteID: 3077, SiteName: 523-05-I. Marker Location Top Reach. LARGE TREE ON RL USOF TR50m to BR, bearing 210°. 8/20/2010

Appendix E. Stream Channel Monitoring Site Photos, JODA 2010 (continued)

John Day, SiteID: 3077, SiteName: 523-05-I. Marker Location Bottom Reach. POWERLINE POLE ON RL30m to BR, bearing 310°. 8/20/2010

John Day, SiteID: 3077, SiteName: 523-05-I. Bottom of reach facing upstream. 8/20/2010

Appendix E. Stream Channel Monitoring Site Photos, JODA 2010 (continued)

John Day, SiteID: 3077, SiteName: 523-05-I. Bottom of reach facing downstream. 8/20/2010

NPS 177/109164, August 2011